A Gift of

The Wellesley
Free Library
Centennial Fund

DOLPHINS

LIVING WILD

Published by Creative Education

P.O. Box 227, Mankato, Minnesota 56002

Creative Education is an imprint of The Creative Company

Design and production by Mary Herrmann

Art direction by Rita Marshall

Printed in the United States of America

Photographs by Dreamstime (Djodlight, Kenm, Photodesign, Pjmorley, Pwozza), Getty Images (De Agostini, Georgette Douwma, Fred Felleman, Gallo Images-Rod Haestier, Flip Nicklin, Gail Shumway, Stuart Westmorland, Norbert Wu), iStockphoto (Brett Atkins, Lars Christensen, Mike Coverdale, Mikael Damkier, Franky De Meyer, Jose Manuel Gelpi Diaz, Ana Druga, Andreas Edelmann, Keith Flood, Jose Gil, Benjamin Jessop, Nancy Nehring, Tammy Peluso, Michael Price, Kristian Sekulic, Krzysztof Slusarczyk, James Steidl, Adam White, Tammy Wolfe)

Library of Congress Cataloging-in-Publication Data

Skog, Jason.

Dolphins / by Jason Skog.

p. cm. — (Living wild)

Includes index.

ISBN 978-1-58341-653-2

1. Dolphins—Juvenile literature. I. Title. II. Series.

QL 737.C432S56 2008

599.53—dc22   2007008500

First Edition

9 8 7 6 5 4 3 2 1

© CREATIVE EDUCATION

DOLPHINS

Jason Skog

The sun is setting, and a group of dolphins is chasing a massive ship

as it sails across the ocean.

The sun is setting, and a group of dolphins is chasing a massive ship as it sails across the ocean. They are racing to the front where the waves break off the ship's bow. As the dolphins catch up, they slip into the foamy curl, riding it like surfers catching a wave. They leap out of the water, flipping their sleek, gray bodies in the air, and dive back in to search for food. One of the dolphins spots a school of

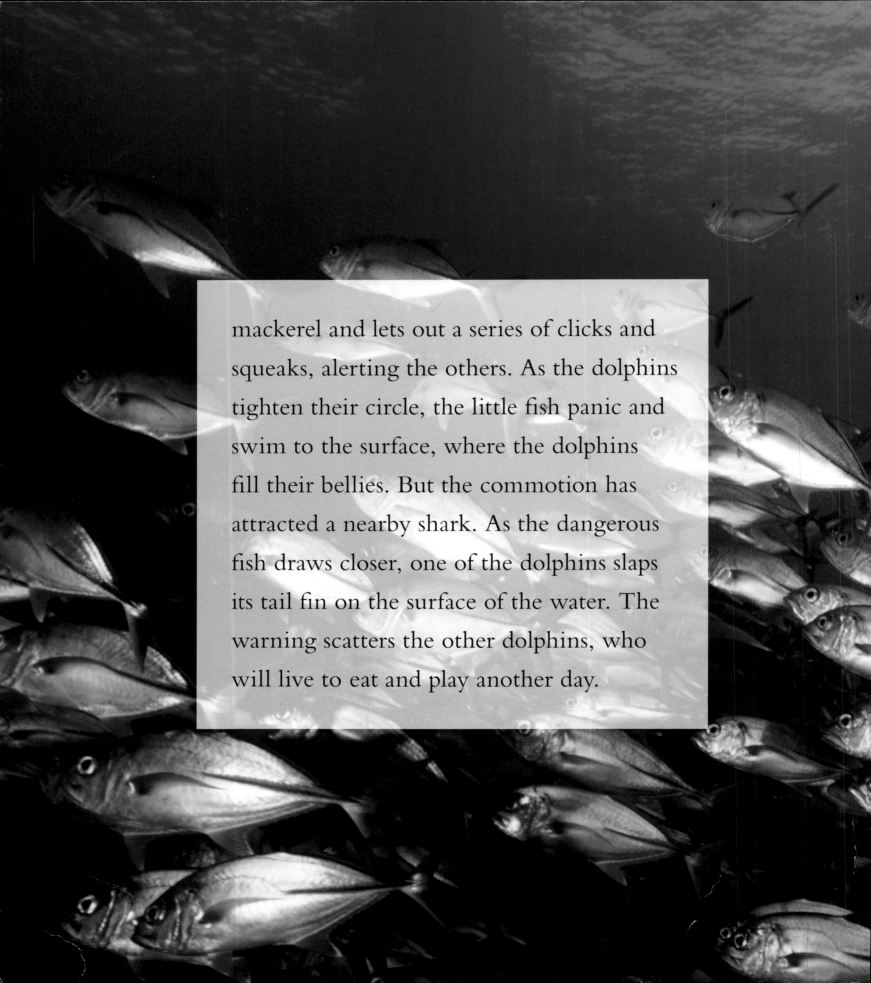

mackerel and lets out a series of clicks and squeaks, alerting the others. As the dolphins tighten their circle, the little fish panic and swim to the surface, where the dolphins fill their bellies. But the commotion has attracted a nearby shark. As the dangerous fish draws closer, one of the dolphins slaps its tail fin on the surface of the water. The warning scatters the other dolphins, who will live to eat and play another day.

WHERE IN THE WORLD THEY LIVE

■ **Common Dolphin**
coastal waters
of North and
South America,
western Europe,
and New Zealand,
Mediterranean Sea

■ **Bottlenose Dolphin**
Atlantic, Pacific,
and Indian oceans

■ **Killer Whale**
Antarctic, northern
Atlantic, and
coastal Pacific
oceans

■ **Spinner Dolphin**
Middle Atlantic
and Pacific oceans,
Indian Ocean

■ **Short-finned Pilot
Whale**
Atlantic, Pacific,
and Indian oceans

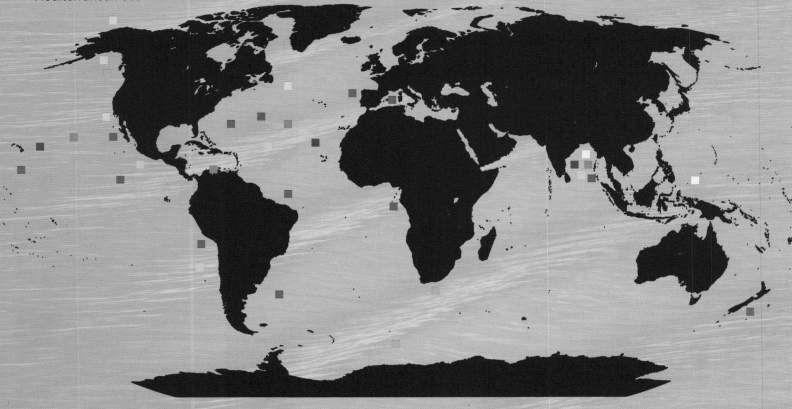

The 32 species of dolphin may be
found in all of Earth's oceans and
seas (with the exceptions of the
Caspian and Aral seas), and some
dolphins even live in freshwater
rivers. The colored dots roughly
represent the ranges of eight
well-known dolphin species.

■ **Rough-toothed
Dolphin**
Atlantic, Pacific,
and Indian oceans,
Caribbean Sea

■ **Right Whale
Dolphin**
North Pacific
Ocean, all waters
between southern
tip of Africa and
Antarctica

■ **Humpbacked
Dolphin**
coastal waters
of Indian Ocean,
western Pacific
Ocean between
China and Australia

SIZES, SHAPES, AND SURROUNDINGS

D olphins are among the ocean's most intelligent, curious, and fascinating creatures. They have attracted attention and inspired artists, mythologists, and ordinary people alike for centuries. The animals continue to attract scientific study, surprise and delight audiences, and challenge human perceptions about their lives.

There are at least 32 species of dolphin, and they vary greatly in size, shape, and color. There are, however, some traits that all dolphins share. They all have conical teeth, slender, streamlined bodies, and pronounced, beak-like snouts.

Dolphins belong to the Delphinidae family, the largest family of the Cetacea order. Dolphins are known as cetaceans (*suh-TAY-shuns*), a group which also includes whales and porpoises. Because they are related, dolphins and whales share some traits. But most whales are much larger than dolphins. Whales also have different behaviors and feeding habits. Porpoises are close cousins to dolphins, but they are usually much smaller in size.

Like whales, dolphins have a single blowhole on top

Much like humans, dolphins have sensitive and delicate skin that can be damaged by bumping into rough objects.

Unlike dolphins, sea lions can both swim and move about on land.

Like a cow, a dolphin has two stomachs. The first stomach stores the food, while the second stomach digests it.

of their heads, slightly to the left of the middle. They use the blowhole to breathe. When they swim to the surface, they quickly breathe out through their blowholes and breathe in just before diving back below the surface. Because dolphins breathe **voluntarily**, they have to think about when to surface so that they can exhale and inhale. Living in the water but needing air to breathe means they can't sleep like land animals. Dolphins float near the surface and "doze," breathing less deeply and swimming more slowly than usual.

Dolphins make their homes in oceans, seas, gulfs, and bays around the world. Some even swim up rivers and live in freshwater environments. Dolphins are social animals. They are not exclusive. They have been spotted swimming alongside such creatures as sea lions, turtles, and eels.

Dolphins may live in water, but they are not fish. They are marine, or sea, mammals, and they breathe air as humans and other animals do. They also give birth to live babies instead of hatching eggs, and mother dolphins feed their young with milk.

Dolphins are warm-blooded. Their body temperature stays about the same no matter the temperature of their

When a dolphin exhales, the air leaves the blowhole at speeds upwards of 100 miles (161 km) per hour.

surroundings. Some like cooler water, while others thrive where it is warmer. But most dolphins prefer temperate or tropical waters where surface temperatures are between 50 and 90 °F (10 to 32 °C). While some dolphins will live in the deeper waters of the open ocean, most prefer to live closer to shore, usually within 100 miles (161 km) of the coastline.

Near shore, dolphins rarely remain below the surface for more than three or four minutes, and they breathe about once or twice per minute on average. But some dolphins can hold their breath for as long as 10 minutes, allowing them to swim to deeper and darker parts of the ocean. After analyzing the contents of some dolphins' stomachs,

When a dolphin exhales, the air leaves the blowhole at speeds upwards of 100 miles (161 km) per hour.

Spinner dolphins live in groups ranging from less than 10 to groups numbering in the thousands.

scientists concluded that some dolphins dive more than a quarter mile (.4 km) below the surface to eat fish that live only at depths of 1,500 feet (457 m). As a dolphin dives to such depths, the water pressure becomes incredible. To adapt, a dolphin's lungs will **compress**, and its heartbeat will slow down until it can return closer to the surface.

A dolphin's color, size, and shape can vary, depending on where it lives. Those that live closer to shore are generally smaller and lighter in color with larger fins. Dolphins that live in the deeper seas are typically larger and darker in color with smaller fins.

Among the 32 known species, dolphins can be as short as 4 feet (1.2 m) and as long as 30 feet (9.1 m). The smallest can weigh less than 100 pounds (45.4 kg), while the largest— the killer whale—can weigh more than 10 tons (9 t).

The common bottlenose dolphin is what most people picture when they think of a dolphin. Bottlenose dolphins are also called gray porpoises, black porpoises, Atlantic or Pacific bottlenose dolphins, or cowfish. A bottlenose dolphin measures about 8 to 12 feet long (2.4–3.7 m). Females weigh about 600 pounds (272 kg), but males can weigh more than 1,000 pounds (454 kg). Most bottlenose

To keep moving at fast speeds, dolphins jump out of the water to save energy.

A dolphin will sometimes use its tail to knock a fish out of shallow water and onto a sandbar in order to catch it.

A bottlenose dolphin's many teeth are designed more to help it grasp food than to chew it.

dolphins sport a silvery gray color that is a slightly darker shade on its top side than its belly.

Dolphins have a beak-like nose and cone-shaped teeth. The length and width of their beak, or nose, also depends on the species. Some species' are very long and narrow. Others are short and fat. Some don't have much of a beak at all. Bottlenose dolphins have a distinct, medium-sized beak. The shape of the bottlenose dolphin's beak also contributes to the shape of its mouth, which turns up slightly at the corners, making the bottlenose appear as though it has a permanent grin.

All dolphins have a prominent dorsal fin, which is the tall, triangular fin in the middle of the back. They also have a notched fluke, or tail fin, and a flipper on either side toward the front of their bodies. Tail flippers help dolphins move through the water, while the side flippers and dorsal fins help them steer.

Dolphins' streamlined shape and smooth skin reduce friction in the water, allowing them to swim faster than many other ocean creatures. Dolphins also have a thick layer of blubber, or fat, around their bodies that protects them from drastic changes in water temperature. And dolphins are extremely flexible. Some of the bones in their necks are not connected to the rest of their backbone. This allows a dolphin to turn its head at a 90-degree angle to its body, an impossible feat for most of its relatives.

Most dolphins **migrate** hundreds or even thousands of miles each year, depending on where they live. In the Northern Hemisphere, dolphins swim north to feed in the summer and south to breed in the winter. In the Southern Hemisphere, it is the opposite. They swim toward the South Pole to feed in the cooler waters during the summer. And in the winter, dolphins swim north toward the equator to breed.

Some species of dolphin have dorsal fins that curve back, while others' stand straight up.

Most dolphins swallow their prey whole. But with larger fish, dolphins have been known to bite the heads off before swallowing the body.

Young dolphins will swim close to their mothers, who will put themselves in danger to save their young.

LIVING, LOVING, AND LEARNING TOGETHER

With a typical lifespan of 25 years, dolphins are some of the ocean's longest-living creatures. Some males can live as long as 45 years and some females as long as 50 years. Male dolphins are called bulls, while female dolphins are called cows. A dolphin's mating season takes place in the spring and early summer. Much is known about dolphins' reproductive systems and habits because they have been studied in aquariums and the wild for so long.

When mating begins, a male will pursue the female with a lot of head bumping. Once the two have mated, the one-year **gestation** period begins. Females almost always give birth to only one dolphin, and baby dolphins are called calves. When a dolphin is born, it comes out tail-first—the only mammal in the world to do so. The young dolphin is about three and a half feet (1 m) long, about a third the length of its mother. After birth, calves quickly swim to the surface for their first breath of air.

Calves drink their mother's milk for 18 to 20 months before they begin eating on their own. Then they remain

Two Atlantic spotted dolphins engage in courtship behavior.

During courtship, male and female dolphins will rub their bellies together or touch flippers, making it look as if they are "holding hands."

A group of dolphins, called a pod, will work together to round up a school of fish so all can feed.

near their protective mothers for up to six years, learning how to hunt and feed. Mothers can give birth about every 3 years from the time they are between ages 5 and 10 until they die. Some females in the wild have given birth when they were 45 years old.

Female dolphins live in groups and may stay together for years, courted by a variety of adult males. They seek

food and raise their young together. They also protect one another from **predators**. Males tend to swim near females and their young, even though the males do not help raise the calves.

The size and makeup of dolphin groups depend on where the dolphins live. Those that live in bays often form smaller groups of anywhere from 2 to 15 dolphins.

Although they are members of the dolphin family, killer whales are occasional predators of bottlenose dolphins.

Dolphins in larger areas offshore can form groups that range from dozens to hundreds.

Apart from dolphins' ability to hunt together, which seems to be the main reason they live in groups, ease of reproduction is another. If more dolphins live together, they have a better chance of finding mates and having calves. A group of dolphins also has better odds protecting young dolphins than does a single mother working by herself. In fact, when a dolphin is born, adults form a circle around the mother because the scent of birth can attract sharks.

When dolphins are threatened by predators such as sharks or killer whales, they work together to fend off an attack. They will help those in their group that are injured or in trouble, lifting them to the surface with their flippers and fins so they can get a breath of air.

Despite dolphins' peaceful, friendly image, they can be aggressive. Some have been spotted chasing and butting into smaller dolphins and porpoises competing for food or mates. Sometimes they can knock other animals completely out of the water using this tactic.

Excellent swimming skills are a dolphin's best defense against attackers such as its main predator, the shark. Many dolphins can swim as fast as 25 miles (40 km) per hour, but only for a short time. Faster and more agile than most sharks, dolphins often escape before they can be injured.

A dolphin's ability to communicate also helps it to live in groups and work with other dolphins. Using a series of clicks and whistles called phonations, dolphins can warn others about approaching danger or let them know

While a shark is a dolphin's most dangerous predator, dolphins have been known to chase sharks away or even kill them.

Dolphins will play with whatever materials are available in their ocean homes, including sea grass.

food is near. Some sounds may even communicate that a dolphin is hurt or lost. Out of the water, dolphins hear through tiny pinholes on the sides of their head. Under water, dolphins rely on a soft spot on the front of their head to locate sound.

Dolphins make noises using air-filled sacs connected to their blowholes. When a dolphin clicks or squeaks, the sound waves bounce off an object—such as a fish, boat, the ocean floor, or other dolphins—and travel back to the dolphin, creating a "picture" of sound. A dolphin can then identify the object depending on how fast the sound bounces back, or echoes, and how the sound has changed. In some studies, blindfolded dolphins have been able to locate and find differences in objects as small as coins. The system—called echolocation—helps dolphins find their way around the ocean, especially in deeper, darker waters.

Dolphins' behavior sets them apart from almost every other creature in the ocean. They are playful, social, and smart animals. Scientists have compared a dolphin's spinning, twisting, chasing, and leaping to the movements of children playing during recess. Dolphins will chase one another as though they are playing tag. They swim

Dolphins can be trained to "stand" on their tails.

Every dolphin's dorsal fin is unique. The fins help dolphins recognize one another, much like people recognize individual faces.

A pod of dolphins keep themselves amused by leaping through the water, trying to outdistance one another.

in circles, jump over each other, flip, and frolic. They have been seen tussling with seaweed, scooping pebbles and rocks in their mouths, or balancing objects they find on their flippers. Some have been known to carry objects around in their mouths, making it look as if they are playing "keep away" from other dolphins.

When it comes to finding a meal, dolphins need to satisfy a big appetite. Most dolphins feed on fish that swim together in large groups called schools. When searching for food, dolphins space themselves apart in a wide line or a U shape as they move through the water. When one of them finds fish, it signals to the others. The dolphins then circle the school of fish and herd them together before eating them.

A common bottlenose dolphin eats 15 to 30 pounds (7–14 kg) of food a day. Those that live closer to shore eat foods found on the seafloor, including squids and **crustaceans** such as crabs. Dolphins in deeper waters feed on a variety of fish, including croakers, sea trout, mackerel, and mullet. Although it is rare, a dolphin may hunt independently if it is especially hungry or if prey presents itself.

Because a dolphin's teeth aren't meant for chewing, it swallows small prey such as fish whole.

Dolphin trainers at theme parks and zoos teach the animals tricks such as jumping through hoops.

FAST FRIENDS

Dolphins have fascinated humans for centuries. Perhaps it is because their short, upturned mouth makes it seem as if they are always smiling. Or maybe it is because they are so curious. Dolphins have been known to swim close to humans, playfully splash them, and even rescue them if they are drowning. People who have spent time near dolphins in the water say the animals are very gentle and patient with humans. They will swim close enough to be touched and scratched and may even take a person along for a fast swim.

There are times, however, when dolphins are not interested in being near people. In those cases, a dolphin might nudge a person with its beak enough to push him or her out of the water. It may even open its mouth and scratch with its teeth to discourage someone from coming near.

Bottlenose dolphins seem especially interested in people and man-made objects. One of their favorite activities is swimming alongside large, powerful ships as they move through the ocean. They will swim ahead of or beside a ship and ride the waves created by the back

Dolphins have exceptional eyesight and hearing but lack the nerves needed to give them a sense of smell.

The killer whale is the largest member of the dolphin family at 30 feet (9 m) long.

of the ship. If they find the right spot, dolphins can ride a wave without having to paddle, much like surfers on surfboards.

The bigger the boat, the larger the wave it creates. That can attract a whole group of dolphins. In New Zealand, a dolphin known as "Pelorus Jack" rode the waves of vessels sailing into port for more than 20 years. Sailors believed that Jack helped guide them through the dangerous, rocky waters of the French Pass, a channel separating mainland New Zealand from D'Urville Island. Jack was last seen in 1912.

Dolphins are incredibly curious and intelligent animals. Studies have shown that dolphins are among the world's smartest animals—perhaps even smarter than chimpanzees or dogs. Such intelligence has made them ideal to train, and dolphin acts have become popular attractions at zoos, aquariums, and amusement parks.

Bottlenose dolphins are the most common species seen in **captivity**. Some are trained to repeat many of the same behaviors they exhibit in the wild. During a show, dolphins are rewarded with fish for their tricks. Some dolphins can jump through hoops, throw a ball through

ARION'S SONG

Poseidon, though the ruler of the seas, was all alone.

No love, no warmth, no gentleness to soothe his savage soul.

Amphitrite was the nymph he loved.

Any wind would bring her scent.

Any dream would hold her voice, her form and

Any time he woke he found that it was but illusion.

Poseidon, though a god, could not confess

His passion or his frailty or his tenderness.

And so she left, the nymph he loved.

She wandered far away from him.

She never saw his gentle side.

She thought his lust was just a rude intrusion.

Poseidon, though so powerful, was but meek.

Fearful of rejection, shame, and fearful of defeat.

A dolphin left to find the nymph,

He told her of Poseidon's love,

He showed her gentleness and care,

He carried her away from self-imposed seclusion.

Poseidon, though so lonely, was so real.

He learned that, god or man, we must say what we feel.

Amphitrite came on dolphin back.

They looked into each other's eyes.

They made their vow for all of time and

They loved the dolphin for resolving their confusion.

Anonymous

Whether they are hunting or just swimming together, dolphins enjoy the company of each other.

a net, or appear to "walk" on the water by flapping their strong flukes and pointing their bodies straight up in the air. Some can jump 20 feet (6 m) out of the water to ring a bell or snatch a fish from a trainer's mouth. They might also perform flips, spins, or twists and finish with a belly flop that splashes water onto the audience.

But keeping dolphins in captivity is a **controversial** issue. Some people believe it is cruel because the dolphins are stuck in relatively small pools and will never experience their natural home in the ocean. Dolphins kept in captivity generally do not live as long as they would in the ocean. Still, some say featuring dolphins in such shows lets people see how special dolphins are, which may inspire them to protect the animal's natural habitat. Other programs use only rescued and **rehabilitated** dolphins that they say probably would not survive if returned to the ocean.

The showy antics of dolphins in their natural habitat caught the ancient Greeks' attention. They considered dolphins **sacred**, and as early as 300 B.C., dolphins were featured on Greek coins, pottery, paintings, and walls. From the Greeks, sailors around the world learned to trust dolphins, and the animal's presence near a ship was believed to mean a smooth voyage. Among the many Greek **myths** about dolphins, such as the story recounted in an ancient poem called "Arion's Song," most involve dolphins saving people from drowning

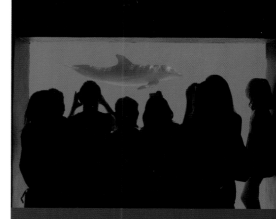

People can pay to see dolphins up close in enclosed underwater tanks at aquariums and zoos.

Some dolphins will herd their prey into shallow waters close to beaches to make feeding easier.

In the 1960s, a dolphin was the star of the popular movie and television series *Flipper*. In 1996, *Flipper* was remade with actor Elijah Wood. *Flipper*, about a young boy's adventures with a dolphin that performed tricks and rescued people, led to the creation of many "dolphinariums" around the United States. These were places that featured captive dolphins that performed tricks. More recently, dolphins have appeared in children's books, novels, music videos, and video games such as "Ecco the Dolphin." Perhaps the most famous dolphins today are not known for their swimming at all. They are the National Football League's Miami Dolphins of Miami, Florida, a team whose helmets feature a picture of a leaping dolphin.

But the relationship between people and dolphins has not always been so close or entertaining. Dolphins in the Pacific Ocean west of Mexico and Central America like to follow commercial fishing and shrimp boats, scooping up injured fish or tasty morsels that the nets may have missed. It is a dangerous practice, and each year, thousands of dolphins are killed by the large gill nets meant for yellowfin tuna. Fishermen searching for tuna will sometimes cast their nets where dolphins have been sighted, since the two animals often swim close to each other. The dolphins then become entangled in the nets' webbing and drown.

Japanese fishermen continue to **harpoon** hundreds of dolphins each year. Thousands more dolphins are killed in places such as the West Indies, Venezuela, Peru, Chile, the Philippines, and Sri Lanka. Dolphins have traditionally been considered food sources in such places, and people use their blubber for oil.

Dolphins can be spotted all over the world. They can be seen swimming along a beach, near a harbor cruise, or close to busy ferry crossings. Special boat tours offer the best chance to catch sight of dolphins because the tours visit areas where the animals are known to gather. In North America, some of the best places to see dolphins in the Pacific Ocean are on Vancouver Island in Canada, off the coast of Southern California, or along the Baja Peninsula in Mexico. The best places to spot dolphins in the Atlantic Ocean are off the coast of Newfoundland in Canada, in the Gulf of St. Lawrence in Canada, along the coast of New England in the U.S., or in the Bahamas.

Many people wonder how animals as intelligent as dolphins are could still be subjected to hunting.

Dolphins' thick, streamlined bodies have adapted to living in the water over millions of years.

FUN WITH SCIENCE

Scientists have long been intrigued by dolphins and continue to uncover new information about the animals' physical makeup and behavior patterns. Dolphins are **descendants** of cetaceans that first appeared more than 50 million years ago. Those marine mammals were skinny swimmers with tiny front flippers and long snouts that lived in coastal waters as well as deep seas.

As dolphins have evolved, so has their intelligence. Scientists have tried to establish how smart dolphins are. A dolphin's brain is roughly the same size as that of a human's. Whether that means they are as smart as humans remains the subject of much debate among scientists.

Dolphins show great ability to mimic behaviors of humans and other animals. In one case, a captive dolphin imitated the behavior of a diver who was cleaning its tank. The dolphin took a stick in its mouth and rubbed it up and down on the glass surface the diver had been cleaning. In another case, a dolphin was allowed to swim with a cape fur seal, and the dolphin soon began imitating the seal's actions. The dolphin groomed itself

Dolphins cannot drink the water they swim in because it is salty. They get the fresh water they need from the fish they eat.

like a seal, swam on its side with one flipper in the air like a seal, and even pretended to sleep on its back like a seal.

Dolphins held in captivity will also invent games and play with nearly anything in their tanks, including feathers, bits of shell, inner tubes, and beach chairs. Their games also often involve humans, whether they are mimicking divers in their tanks or teasing trainers by tossing objects at them. Scientists believe the reason for such behavior is that dolphins in captivity often are bored. Since they don't have to work hard for their food or protect themselves from predators, they keep active by having fun.

In the wild, too, dolphins seem to enjoy playing. Some scientists have suggested that play is part of the development process for younger dolphins. Play helps dolphins learn how to become better swimmers, chase food, and evade predators. Others believe play helps dolphins connect with one another and form stronger social groups.

Adult dolphins can develop very strong attachments to each other. In one study, a female dolphin was held in captivity for 10 years with another male. When the two

A bottlenose dolphin constantly makes sounds such as whistles and squawks that humans can hear.

Dolphins that appear to be silent while swimming may actually be communicating at higher frequencies.

were separated, the female refused to perform tricks for her trainers. For two days and three nights she swam in the middle of her tank, bobbing her head up and down and screeching. She paid no attention to her normal toys, except to flip them violently out of her tank. When her tank mate returned, she resumed her normal behavior.

Studies have suggested that each dolphin seems to have a unique click or squeal, much like a human voice. But dolphins make many more sounds humans cannot hear because human ears are not sensitive enough. Scientists are still unsure as to what all of the clicks and squeaks mean, but they hope to decipher the dolphins' "language" someday.

Dolphins can be found in oceans throughout the world and can adapt to a variety of habitats. However, some species in certain regions are at risk of disappearing because their habitat is changing so quickly. Areas where pollution and fishing are out of control put dolphins in the greatest danger. Marine debris, such as garbage and discarded fishing nets, also poses a threat to dolphins, as they may confuse the garbage for food and get sick or, worse, become stuck in the nets and be unable to surface for air.

Off the coast of the eastern U.S., dolphin populations suffered a serious setback in the 1920s when many were killed because the dolphins were eating the same fish commercial fishermen were trying to catch. Today, dolphins are protected by the Marine Mammal Protection Act of 1972. The law bans, with few exceptions, the killing of dolphins and other marine mammals such as whales and sea lions in U.S. waters or by U.S. citizens on the high seas. It also does not allow any dolphin or marine mammal products to be brought into the country.

Dolphin populations can also suffer from exposure to viruses and **toxins**. Some scientists believe dolphins are especially vulnerable today because the heavy doses of pollutants from illegal dumping, industrial wastes, and oil spills may have weakened their immune systems. Yet, perhaps the biggest danger facing dolphins is themselves. When they swim too close to shore and get stuck on the sand, dolphins become stranded, or beached. A beached dolphin cannot survive out of the water very long. Without water, the air and sun become too intense, and the animal overheats, even in cool weather. Every year, thousands of dolphins die from stranding.

Garbage such as plastic six-pack rings can end up in the oceans, harming dolphins.

Because dolphins "sleep" with one eye open, they are able to rest while still staying awake enough to swim.

Rescue workers do all they can to save a dolphin that has been beached.

The U.S. Navy trains dolphins to assist human divers in warding off sharks, finding mines, and retrieving or marking objects.

Scientists are not sure why so many dolphins beach themselves. Some scientists believe dolphins can detect the earth's magnetic field, or the force at all points created by the pull on Earth's **magnetic poles**, and use it for direction. When that magnetic field is disrupted or switches unexpectedly, it could cause a dolphin to get lost and swim into shallow waters, where it can easily be washed ashore. Some dolphins occasionally strand themselves with a group of other dolphins. Such mass strandings can occur if the group is following a leader who has become sick or lost. Dolphins that become disoriented or frightened by earthquakes or big storms can easily get lost and strand themselves. Other times they can get stranded if they stop to rest and fail to move on quickly enough.

While they are generally plentiful, dolphin populations are in severe decline in some areas, particularly in Asian oceans, where commercial fishing continues to pose problems for the animal. Authorities around the world continue adopting new laws designed to protect dolphins from intentional or accidental death from fishing and pollution. At the same time, more consumers are

paying closer attention to dolphins, buying "dolphin-safe" products, and industries are becoming increasingly sensitive to dolphin habitats. By changing human behaviors toward dolphins, people will ensure that the fascinating, frolicking, and fun-loving creatures will be around for a long time to come.

Dolphins enjoy riding the waves, whether they are close to shorelines or in the wake of big boats.

ANIMAL TALE: ARION AND THE DOLPHIN

Ancient Greece produced some of the earliest stories about dolphins. Greek sailors were fascinated by dolphins and considered themselves lucky when a dolphin swam near their ship. The following tale shows how dolphins became a popular image in Greek art and provided the inspiration for the constellation of stars known as Delphinus.

Long ago in the land of Greece, there lived a young man named Arion. Arion was the greatest harp player in the land, and he played at King Periander's palace in Corinth.

Everyone knew who Arion was, and everyone admired his talents. But after playing for Periander for many years, Arion realized he was homesick. He asked the king if he could return home to visit his family and friends.

Periander agreed to let him go, and the king himself prepared a ship for Arion's journey there and back.

The sailors aboard the ship, however, were jealous of Arion's wealth and fame. They saw all the trunks of riches that Arion brought with him on the ship, and the evil sailors came up with a plan to rob him once they were out on the open sea. When asked about Arion's disappearance, they planned to say there had been an accident and that he had fallen overboard. That would allow the men to split Arion's riches among themselves.

During the voyage, the god Apollo came to Arion in a dream and warned him about the sailors' plot. The next day, the sailors surrounded Arion. They gave him a choice: He could be taken to land and be killed and

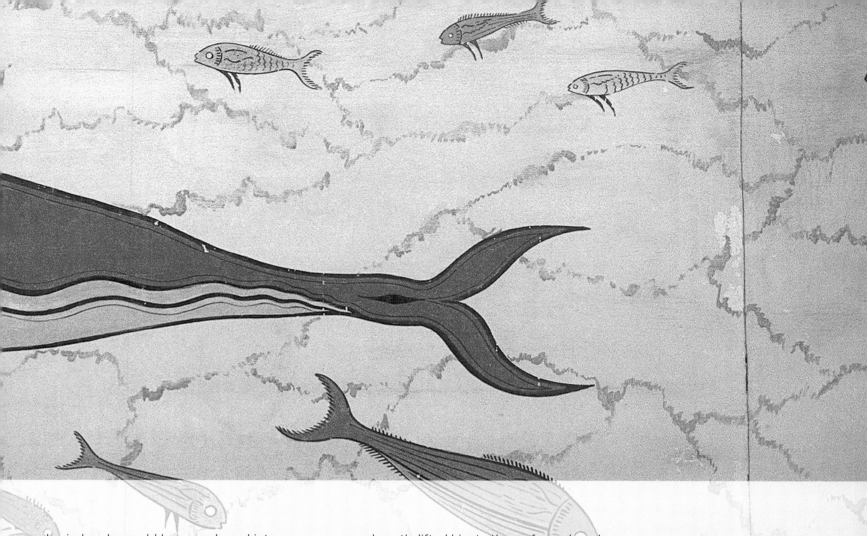

buried, or he could leap overboard into the sea.

"Please grant me one last wish," Arion begged the sailors. "Let me only play a song for you, then you may kill me." The sailors laughed at his request, but they allowed him to play. Arion began singing and playing one of the most beautiful songs they had ever heard. It was lively and high-pitched, and the words praised Apollo, god of music and the arts. Apollo heard the song and was pleased.

The moment Arion finished his tune, he leapt into the waters below and sunk beneath the surface as the sailors quickly sailed away. But Apollo was watching the whole time. He called for a dolphin to rescue Arion, and one soon swam to the spot where Arion had disappeared. The dolphin dived beneath Arion

and gently lifted him to the surface where he could breathe.

The dolphin carried Arion on its back to the kingdom of Taenarum, where Arion swam to shore. Meanwhile, the ship's crew had already returned to Corinth and explained Arion's disappearance. When Arion suddenly arrived at the palace days later, they were shocked to see the man alive and well. After learning the true story, the king put the sailors in prison and forced them to give Arion back his riches.

Arion was grateful to Apollo for sparing his life, so he made a small statue of a dolphin and put it in Apollo's temple to honor his experience. Apollo was so pleased at Arion's rescue that he placed the dolphin in the stars for all to see.

GLOSSARY

captivity – when an animal lives in a tank at a zoo or in an aquarium and not in the wild

compress – to reduce in size by squeezing

controversial – marked by strong and opposing opinions

crustaceans – aquatic invertebrates such as crabs, lobsters, and shrimp, which have a shell, mouth, antenna, and appendages

descendants – individuals that come from a species that lived long ago

gestation – the period of time it takes a baby to develop inside a mother's womb

harpoon – a barbed spear used to hunt large fish or marine mammals

magnetic poles – the two points on Earth, near the North and South Poles, where the earth's magnetic field is the most intense

migrate – to travel from one region or climate to another for feeding or breeding purposes

myths – traditional stories that explain how certain things came to be

predators – animals that survive by hunting and eating other animals

rehabilitated – to be restored to good health

sacred – something religious or worthy of respect

toxins – poisonous substances that can cause illness or death

voluntarily – done on purpose with free will

SELECTED BIBLIOGRAPHY

Carwardine, Mark. *Whales, Dolphins and Porpoises.* New York: Smithsonian Handbooks/ DK Publishing, 2002.

Ellis, Richard. *Dolphins and Porpoises.* New York: Alfred A. Knopf, 1989.

Evans, Peter G. H. *The Natural History of Whales and Dolphins.* New York: Facts on File, 1987.

Lilly, John C. *Communication between Man and Dolphin.* New York: Crown Publishers, 1978.

Reeves, Randall R., Brent S. Stewart, Phillip J. Clapham, and James A. Powell. *National Audubon Society's Guide to Marine Mammals of the World.* New York: Alfred A. Knopf, 2002.

World Book Encyclopedia. 22 vols. Chicago: World Book, 2005.

The graceful image of dolphins leaping out of the water continues to captivate people around the world.

INDEX

behavior 23, 25–26, 29, 37–38, 40
　mimicking others 37–38

bottlenose dolphins 10, 15–16, 26, 29, 30,
　　32–33, 34, 37–38
　in captivity 30, 32–33, 34, 37–38
　names for 15
　physical characteristics 15–16

breathing 12, 13

breeding and mating 17, 19, 22

calves 19–20, 21, 22, 23, 38
　birth 19, 23
　learning behaviors 19–20
　physical characteristics 19
　playing 38

cetaceans 11, 37

communication 8, 23, 25, 40
　echolocation 25
　and hearing 25
　noises 25, 40
　phonations 23
　purposes 23, 25

cultural influences 30, 31, 33, 34, 44–45
　Greek 31, 33, 44
　　Arion's Song 31, 33, 45
　　mythology 31, 33, 44–45
　modern entertainment 34
　　Flipper 34
　　Miami Dolphins 34
　　video games 34
　Pelorus Jack 30

dangers faced 34–35, 40–42
　beaching 41–42
　garbage 40
　gill nets 34–35
　harpooning 35
　over-fishing 40, 42
　pollution 40
　used for blubber 35

Delphinidae family 11

Delphinus constellation 44

dorsal fins 8, 16–17, 25

feeding 15, 17, 26

flippers 17, 19, 23, 26, 37, 38

groups 20–22, 23, 26, 38, 42
　hunting 22, 26, 38
　playing 38
　protecting one another 21, 22, 23, 38

habitats 12, 13, 15, 21–22, 26, 33, 40

intelligence 30, 37

life expectancy 19

mammals 12, 19, 37, 42
　characteristics of 12

migration patterns 10, 17

parent-child relationship 19–20

physical characteristics 11–12, 15–17, 29

populations 40, 42

predators 8, 15, 21, 23, 30, 38
　defensive tactics against 23
　killer whales 15, 23, 30
　sharks 8, 23

protective measures 41, 42

relationships with humans 29–30, 33, 34

relatives 11, 15, 23, 42
　porpoises 11, 15, 23
　whales 11, 42

roles of bulls and cows 19, 20–21

species 11, 15

visiting dolphin habitats 35